DATE DUE

101	reb6/4/10		

WORLD'S WORST...

FIRE
Disasters

Rob Alcraft
Louise Spilsbury

Heinemann Library
Chicago, Illinois

© 2000 Reed Educational & Professional Publishing
Published by Heinemann Library,
an imprint of Reed Educational & Professional Publishing,
100 N. LaSalle, Suite 1010
Chicago, IL 60602

Customer Service 888-454-2279

Designed by Celia Floyd
Illustrations by David Cuzik (Pennant Illustrations) and Jeff Edwards
Originated by Dot Gradations
Printed by Wing King Tong, in Hong Kong

04 03 02 01 00
10 9 8 7 6 5 4 3 2 1

Library of Congress Cataloging-in-Publication Data
Alcraft, Rob, 1966-
    Fire Disasters / Rob Alcraft, Louise Spilsbury
        p. cm. – (World's worst)
    Includes bibliographical references and index.
    ISBN 1-57572-988-1 (library binding)
    1. Great Fire, London, England, 1666 Juvenile literature.
    2. Great Fire, Chicago, Ill., 1871 Juvenile literature.
    3. Wildfires—Australia—Hobart (Tas.) Juvenile literature. 4. Fire
    prevention Juvenile literature. I. Spilsbury, Louise. II. Title.
    III. Series.
        D24.A43 1999   99-37350
                                                  CIP

Acknowledgments
The Publishers would like to thank the following for permission to reproduce photographs: Tony Stone/Paul Edmondson, p. 4; AKG, p. 5; Tony Stone/Richard Kaylin, p. 6; Corbis-Bettmann/James L. Amos, p. 7; Museum of London, pp. 8, 9, 12; Image Select, p. 13; Corbis-Bettmann, pp. 14, 15, 18; Tony Stone/S. & N. Geary, p. 20; Colorific!/Penny Tweedie, p. 21; Topham Picturepoint/Associated Press, p. 24; Still Pictures/Mark Edwards, p. 25; Tony Stone/Gary Irving, p. 26; Heinemann/Chris Honeywell, p. 27; Rex Features, p. 29.

Cover photograph reproduced with permission of Mitch Kezar/Tony Stone.

Some words are shown in bold, **like this**. You can find out what they mean by looking in the glossary.

Contents

Fire

People have used fire for thousands of years. Fire is our friend. It keeps us warm, makes light for us to see by, and cooks our food. But it can also kill and destroy.

In some parts of the world, farmers use fire to keep wild animals away from their cattle and goats. In the Amazon rain forest, local Amazonian Indians use controlled fires to burn back the trees. When the fire is gone, farmers use the land to grow their crops. Or if they leave the land, new tender shoots grow. When animals come to eat the plants, the Indians hunt them for food.

Amazonian Indians know how to live in the rain forest without ruining it. Sadly, some ranchers burn vast areas of the forest for their cattle. Because of this, the rain forest is in danger of being lost altogether.

Controlled burning of small areas of the rain forest, which is used by the Amazonian Indians, does not hurt the environment.

Deadly weapon

Sometimes fire is used as a weapon of war. In World War II, cities such as Tokyo, Japan, and Dresden, Germany, were fire-bombed. The intention was to destroy the cities. The fire that engulfed Tokyo could be seen 145 miles (240 kilometers) away. It killed more than 200,000 people. In Dresden, the bombing created a scorching 100-mile (160-kilometer) per hour wind as the flames sucked air into the city. The city was destroyed, and more than 400,000 people died.

Dresden was in ruins after fire-bomb attacks during World War II.

Fire disasters

In this book, we'll look at three of the worst fire disasters in history. We will look at how the fires started and how they spread. Through eyewitness accounts and expert reports, we will see what happened and how the fires burned out of control. Are there lessons that we could learn from such disasters?

Nowhere to Hide

Fires can happen almost anywhere. Fire destroys plants and animals in forests and grasslands all over the world. Flames swallow buildings—large and small—in villages, towns, and cities every day. Fires occur under the ground in mines and in underground railways. Fires occur under the sea in tunnels deep below the waves. They can even occur in the air—in airplanes full of highly **inflammable** fuel. Most of the time we are safe. All over the world, extensive fire precautions are taken. But sometimes, despite all the measures taken to prevent fires, accidents happen.

Firefighters at airports use a special foam to put out certain kinds of airplane fires.

Fighting fire

Early firefighters used horse-drawn carts and water poured by hand-pumps or buckets to stop a blaze. Today's modern fire services have breathing apparatus, remote cameras, and lifting equipment. Modern water pumps can shoot thousands of gallons of water onto a fire every minute. Firefighters also use foam and other special substances to stop certain kinds of fires.

Forest fires

Today, forest rangers in larger forest areas watch for fires from special towers. In some places, rangers fly over vast forests or grasslands to check for signs of danger. If there is a fire, highly trained and organized teams use trucks to carry water to put out the flames and bulldozers to clear **firebreaks**. They also use helicopters and planes to drop water.

City fires

Firefighters today are helped by modern materials and building design. Materials—brick, stone, concrete, and metal—are less **combustible** than those used in the past. Modern safety standards ensure that public buildings have **fire doors** and **fire extinguishers**. Buildings are also designed so that fire cannot spread quickly through them.

Flash-over

Flash-over is the name for the way a fire can leap through buildings. A flash-over is what happens when the smoke and gas from a fire ignite suddenly in a wall of moving flame. It is one of the most dangerous things a firefighter can face. A flash-over will kill or badly burn anyone in normal clothing. Even the special clothing worn by modern firefighters cannot completely protect them from the intense heat. Firefighters today learn to recognize the signs that can show them a fire is about to flash-over.

Special suits protect today's firefighters from the heat and dangerous fumes given off by most fires.

Devastation!
The Great Fire of London

ENGLAND
London

On Sunday, September 2, 1666, a small fire at a bakery in London grew out of control. The flames ate away at the city for four days. Amazingly, only eight people died. More than half the area within the city walls was destroyed, including 13,200 houses, 87 churches, and most of London's major public buildings.

London

In 1666, London was the second largest city in Europe. Most of its 450,000 inhabitants lived in houses and worked in shops and warehouses. The buildings were built of wood and **thatch** and were packed closely together along narrow streets and alleys. Most people stored wood and other fuel. Everything was dry after a hot summer. London was ready to burn.

This model of London at the time of the Great Fire shows how tightly packed the wooden houses in the city were.

As London burned, many people escaped to the river. They threw their belongings into the river or onto carts as they fled.

Small beginnings

Before going to bed that night, baker Thomas Farrinor made sure that the fires in his ovens were out. But smoldering **embers** ignited wood stored nearby. Around 1:00 A.M., the house was in flames. The family and a servant escaped across the rooftops. The family's maid, fearful of the dangerous climb, stayed behind. She became the first victim of the flames.

The wooden, **pitch**-covered buildings nearby ignited at the touch of the smallest spark. The warehouses along the river were full of **combustible** materials such as timber, oil, and rope. A strong east wind fanned the flames and carried burning embers and debris to other buildings. The fire spread quickly It was almost impossible to fight. The fire chased people from their homes and swallowed everything in its path. By the time the fire was put out on Thursday afternoon, London was in ruins.

Samuel Pepys, a government official in London, kept a famous diary This is taken from his entry for September 2.

(We) stayed there till it was dark almost and saw the fire grow...in corners and upon steeples and between churches and houses as far as we could see up the hill of the City, in a most horrid malicious bloody flame...and a horrid noise the flames made, and the cracking of houses at their ruin.

London's Burning

Londoners were well aware of the risks of fire. In 1630, a fire at an inn stable in Southwark had destroyed 50 houses. In 1633, one third of the houses on London Bridge and 80 nearby had been wrecked by flames. But people in the city thought they were well prepared. Every **parish** was equipped with hooked poles for pulling down burning roofs or houses and pumps, hoses, and leather buckets for **dousing** blazes. But nothing could have prepared them for the **inferno** of 1666.

England

River
Thames

Key
London – present day
London – before 1666 fire

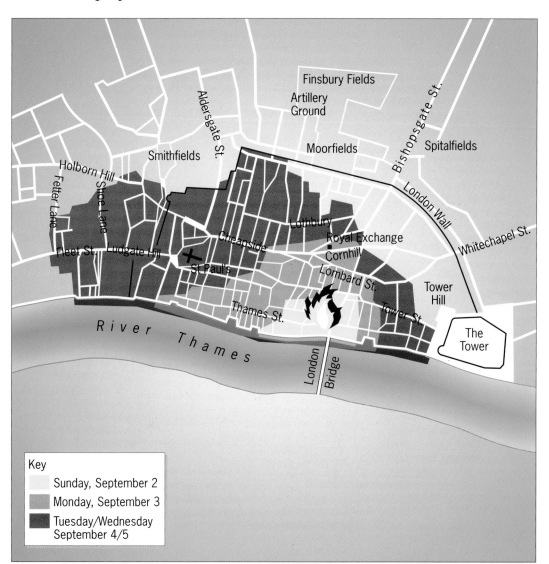

Finsbury Fields
Artillery
Ground
Moorfields
Spitalfields
Smithfields
Aldersgate St.
Bishopsgate St.
Holborn Hill
Shoe Lane
Fetter Lane
London Wall
Whitechapel St.
Lothbury
Cheapside
Royal Exchange
Cornhill
Fleet St.
Ludgate Hill
St Paul's
Lombard St.
Thames St.
Tower St.
Tower Hill
River Thames
London Bridge
The Tower

Key
Sunday, September 2
Monday, September 3
Tuesday/Wednesday
September 4/5

1. Sunday. At about 2:00 A.M., a fire in a bakery spreads to nearby houses. The Lord Mayor, Sir Thomas Bludworth, is alerted. He declares that fire will be easy to put out and that there is no need to pull down houses to make a **firebreak**. The fire spreads to nearby streets and to warehouses along the river. By 4:00 A.M., a strong wind spreads the flames. About 100 houses are burned every hour. Firefighters throw water from buckets, but the heat keeps them from getting very close. King Charles I orders Bludworth to tear down houses to create firebreaks. But many people are reluctant to allow this, and firebreaks are made too close to the front of the fire to be any use. The fire is beyond control. Londoners flee.

2. Monday. Driven by the east wind, the fire moves west towards Fleet River and north beyond Cornhill and the Royal Exchange, the business center of the city. The king puts the Duke of York in charge. His guards organize firebreaks, and try to keep the peace and prevent **looting**.

3. Tuesday morning. **Militia** arrive from outside London to help fight the fire. Cheapside is destroyed, and half the city is in flames. St. Paul's Cathedral is lost to the inferno. Flames up to 330 feet (100 meters) high reach halfway up Fleet Street. Gunpowder is used to clear firebreaks, which save the Tower of London.

4. Wednesday. The fire reaches Temple and Cripplegate, but the wind drops and it goes no further. Although the fire still burns, the improved conditions make it possible to start fighting it. By the end of the day, all fires in the west are extinguished.

5. Thursday. With most of the fires out, all resources are concentrated on the remaining flames. An outbreak at Temple is extinguished by 2:00 A.M. By the end of the day, the Great Fire of London is over—at last.

What Went Wrong?

How did a small fire destroy a city? A committee was set up to investigate. Though the report found that the fire began at Farrinor's bakery, it concluded that the devastation was caused by "the hand of God upon us, a great wind, and the season so very dry."

These Engins, (which are   the best) to quench great Fires; are

Out of control

The wind and the dryness of the season did not explain why the fire was not tackled more efficiently. One reason was that it began in the middle of the night, as people slept. Also, it was Sunday, so fewer people than usual were up early. Action was only taken when the fire had grown too fierce to be controlled. Many people said that Lord Mayor Bludworth was responsible because he did not act as quickly or firmly as he should have. As a result, **firebreaks** were made too late.

Although firefighting equipment, like this engine designed in 1658, was available, it was not much use. It was not used soon enough and it could not carry very much water.

After the fire

Most people had lost everything. 100,000 people spent a harsh winter living in makeshift shelters and tents. Many people had no clothes other than what they were wearing and had nothing to cook with. Churches raised some relief funds, and the government organized financial assistance. But it was a hard winter for many.

After a relatively slow start—only 150 houses were built in the first year—most new building was completed within five years. The new city was a safer and healthier place to live. Houses were made of stone, brick, and tile and were on wider streets with better **sanitation**.

God's punishment?

It was commonly accepted that the fire was God's punishment. A sign on a statue in memory of the disaster read that the fire started as a warning against "the sin of gluttony." A report in *The London Gazette* on September 10 said that the fire was "the heavy hand of God upon us for our sins, showing us the terror of his judgement." When the wind dropped so the fire could be put out, people believed God was at last showing mercy.

After the Great Fire, **architect** Christopher Wren designed 52 new **parish** churches and rebuilt St Paul's Cathedral, now a famous London landmark.

Inferno!
The Chicago Fire of 1871

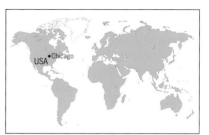

On October 8, 1871, a barn fire in Chicago, Illinois, raged out of control. After two days of destruction, 300 people were dead and 100,000 people were homeless. Offices, public buildings, and factories were wrecked.

Chicago before the fire

In 1871, Chicago was a bustling, vibrant city. Nestled between the manufacturing east and the farming west and linked to both by railroads, Chicago was ideally situated to become a great economic and business center. Goods were made, bought, and sold, all within the city limits.

The branches of the Chicago River divided the city into North, South, and West Divisions. Buildings were made of, or trimmed with, wood. Streets and pavements were lined with wood. Timber was stacked in warehouses along the river. Wooden goods were made in mills and factories. The wooden city was dry after a parched summer that had stretched into the autumn months. Barely 1.6 inches (4 centimeters) of rain had fallen since July.

In 1871, Chicago was on its way to becoming an economic and business center.

This picture, *The Rush for Life over Randolph Steet Bridge, 1871*, was painted from a sketch made during the fire by John R. Chapin.

Fire in the city

Patrick O'Leary, his wife Catherine, and their five children lived at 13 DeKoven Street in the West Division, in the cramped back rooms of a small wooden cottage. Catherine O'Leary ran a milk business from a nearby barn. Although it is not known precisely how the fire started, it seems that sometime around 9:00 P.M. on October 8, 1871, a blaze began in the vicinity of the O'Leary barn. The fire spread quickly, driven by a fierce wind and headed for the city center less than 1 mile (1.6 kilometers) away. People started to panic. Many were crushed in their homes or in the city's tunnels and bridges as they struggled to **evacuate**.

This eyewitness account of the Chicago fire was written by New York **Assemblyman** Alexander Frear, writing in the *New York World* newspaper on October 15, 1871.

Wabash Avenue was utterly choked with all manner of goods and people. Everybody who had been forced from the other end of town by the advancing flames had brought some article with him, and, as further progress was delayed, if not completely stopped by the river—the bridges of which were also choked—most of them, in their panic, abandoned their burdens, so that the streets and sidewalks presented the most astonishing wreck. Valuable oil paintings, books, pet animals, musical instruments, toys, mirrors, and bedding, were trampled underfoot.

A Two-Day Inferno

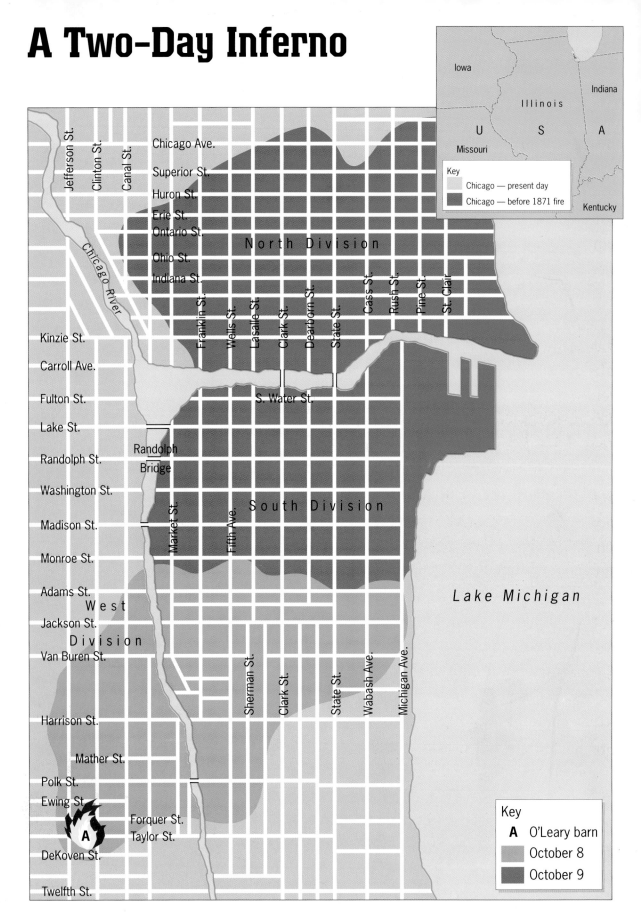

Iowa

Illinois

Indiana

U   S   A

Missouri

Kentucky

Key
- Chicago — present day
- Chicago — before 1871 fire

Jefferson St.
Clinton St.
Canal St.

Chicago Ave.
Superior St.
Huron St.
Erie St.
Ontario St.
Ohio St.
Indiana St.

North Division

Franklin St.
Wells St.
Lasalle St.
Clark St.
Dearborn St.
State St.
Cass St.
Rush St.
Pine St.
St. Clair

Chicago River

Kinzie St.
Carroll Ave.
Fulton St.
Lake St.
Randolph St.
Washington St.
Madison St.
Monroe St.
Adams St.
Jackson St.
Van Buren St.

S. Water St.

Randolph Bridge

Market St.
Fifth Ave.

South Division

West
Division

Lake Michigan

Harrison St.
Mather St.
Polk St.
Ewing St
Forquer St.
Taylor St.
DeKoven St.
Twelfth St.

Sherman St.
Clark St.
State St.
Wabash Ave.
Michigan Ave.

Key
- **A** O'Leary barn
- October 8
- October 9

1. At about 9:00 P.M. on Sunday, October 8, a fire starts near the O'Leary family barn in the West Division. A strong south-westerly wind drives the fire towards the city center. People panic and begin to flee.

2. At around midnight, the wind carries blazing **embers** and smoldering debris onto new buildings to start new fires. Some embers jump across the south branch of the river, sparking more fires on the other side. The city is becoming an **inferno**. The buildings and the wooden streets are all in flames.

3. By 1:30 A.M., the fire reaches the courthouse tower. When officials realize that the building is going to be burned, they release the prisoners. Thousands of people surge towards the North Division to escape, but the fire is catching up with them. The fire is spreading west and north now.

4. By 3:00 A.M., the fire is moving up Huron Street, devouring houses along its burning path. At 3:30 A.M., the pumping station on that street is wrecked, ruining any chances of fighting the fire from the site.

5. By midday on Monday, the fires in the North Division reach North Avenue, then Fullerton Avenue, and then the northern edge of the city.

6. By Tuesday morning, rain starts to fall. The flames are quenched at last. Chicago is left smoldering and devastated.

The Aftermath of Disaster

By the time the fire was finally put out by the rain, two days after it began, it had incinerated a vast area, almost 4 miles (6.5 kilometers) long and over half a mile (1 kilometer) wide. 27 miles (45 kilometers) of streets had been lost, along with 115 miles (192 kilometers) of sidewalks and 18,000 buildings. Survivors—rich and poor—escaped to any safe stretches of land they could find.

Chicago remained scorching hot for almost two days. Newspapers reported that when business owners returned and opened their safes, the money inside, which had survived the **inferno**, burst into flames on contact with the baking hot air. Incredibly, when people did explore the city to assess the damage, they found that although the O'Leary family barn had been reduced to ashes, the cottage was still standing!

Chicago lies in ruins after the fire of 1871.

A preventable disaster?

The Chicago disaster could have been prevented if only the O'Leary barn fire had been extinguished in good time. Chicago firefighters were well-equipped and experienced. The city had suffered and successfully put out an average of two fires a day in the previous year. However, there had been a particularly large fire the night before. Firefighters were exhausted. Perhaps that is why they were slow to respond.

In addition, firefighters alerted to the blaze at the barn were directed to the wrong neighborhood. By the time they reached the O'Leary barn, the fire was way beyond control.

Rebuilding the city

Luckily for the residents of Chicago, the country's developing industries had invested too much time and money in their city to let it die. Chicago still had two of the most important ingredients for future success—location and resources. Within six weeks, rebuilding was well underway. Town planners had learned their lessons from the fire—new homes were divided from factories and offices in the center and were built out of less **combustible** materials.

The hand of God?

No single person was ever convicted of causing the Chicago disaster. Instead, it seems, a series of mistakes and delays was to blame. And, as in the Great Fire of London in 1666, people saw the hand of God at work. The Mayor of Chicago set aside Sunday, October 29 as "a special day of humiliation and prayer; of humiliation for those past offenses against Almighty God, to which these severe afflictions were doubtless intended to lead our minds; of prayer for the relief and comfort of the suffering thousands in our midst; for the restoration of our material prosperity, especially for our lasting improvement as a people in reverence and obedience to God."

Wildfire!

Bushfires in Hobart, Tasmania

Australia
Hobart •
Tasmania

In just under five hours on February 7, 1967, ferocious **bushfires** around Hobart, Tasmania, burned an area of 660,675 acres (264,270 hectares). Over 1,400 homes were destroyed, and 62 people were killed. It was one of the worst fires ever recorded in the history of the country.

An area at risk

Hobart is the capital city of Tasmania, an **island state** of Australia. The city nestles between Mount Wellington and the Derwent River. The river provides a natural harbor. Its shoreline is fringed with picturesque bays and headlands. Hobart is surrounded by large expanses of forest and grassland.

This aerial view shows Hobart and the surrounding area.

Bushfires are a frequent occurence throughout Australia, particularly after droughts. The fires can leave destruction in their wake.

Devastating fires

On Tuesday morning, about 110 small fires burned—some started accidentally, others on purpose. Around 11:00 A.M., a strong wind suddenly fanned these small fires into violent blazes that swept into the Hobart area, across the slopes of Mount Wellington and right down to the edges of the city.

Hillsides seemed to explode when burning **embers**, carried by the wind, showered down. In some places, huge fireballs of burning gas rolled ahead of the main fires, crossing roads and **firebreaks**. Pockets of unburned gas were blown across the sky. When the gas pockets were ignited by smoldering embers, they exploded in mid-air with a deafening roar.

The fire danger index

The hottest months in the Australian summer are January and February. The summer of 1967 had brought severe **drought**, and the Hobart area was parched–ready to be ignited by the slightest spark.

Meteorologists rate the likelihood of fire in a fire danger index. Factors that contribute to risk are drought, high wind speed, high fuel levels (the amount of **combustible** plant life or goods in a region), and low **humidity**. In February 1967, the Hobart region had all of these things, giving it a fire danger index rating of 100—the severest recorded there in 70 years!

21

The Flames Take Hold

The night before had been mild. The early morning air was relatively damp, leaving plantlife in the forested areas quite moist. It took until nearly midday for the trees and grasses to dry out. When they did, what had been small, insignificant fires were stoked into life by changing winds. Disaster unfolded.

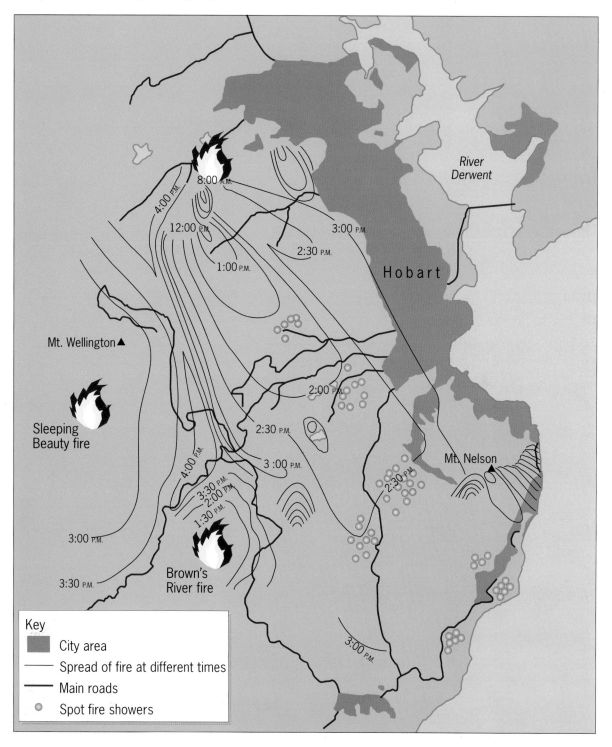

1. Around 11:00 A.M., gale-force winds blow up. Grasses and trees have dried out completely. The Hobart area is extremely hot and dry. Small fires that have been smoldering in the area suddenly burst into violent activity.

2. At 12:00 A.M., fires in the forest country advance, speeded by the wind. Wind-blown **embers** from these forest blazes create **spot fires** ahead of the main fire. Many trees are not completely stripped of leaves because the wind is so strong that it blows out fires in the treetops.

3. After 1:00 P.M., there is a tremendous increase in the amount of land covered by flames. Some fires run into the back of each other to become an ever-advancing wall of flames. The main fires are reaching a peak of destruction. Within two hours—between 1:00 P.M. and 3:00 P.M.—135,000 acres (54,000 hectares) of grassland and forest country are burned.

4. Between 2:00 P.M. and 4:00 P.M., the high winds shift direction dramatically from the southwest to the northeast. This proves to be disastrous. Many fires that were previously separate are now blown together. People are trapped where fires suddenly meet, finding their escape routes barred by more flames, and many are killed. There is nothing standing in the way of the fires blazing in much of the open grassland and areas of small forests. The fires in these regions burn freely.

5. Around 3:00 P.M., severe fire **whirlwinds** develop on the slopes of Mount Wellington. The Hobart and Sleeping Beauty fires start to draw together. The Hobart fire reaches the western edge of the city.

6. By 4:00 P.M., some fires die out when they reach the sea. Others are finally extinguished by firefighters and volunteers.

After the Fire

Over 1,300 homes were wrecked by the fire, as well as 128 major buildings such as factories, churches, and schools. Farmers lost lands and livestock. Communication systems—such as road, rail, and telephone—were wrecked.

After the fire, investigations into its causes began. The Police Department, Hobart City Council, the Forestry Commission, Fire Brigades, and other government authorities joined together. Witnesses were interviewed, and photographs were taken from airplanes to track the progress of the fire. Gradually the pieces of the puzzle that led to the disaster were put together.

Distraught family members survey the ruins of their home.

Children were safe

Incredibly, no children or young people were killed by the Hobart fires. Most were at School at the peak time of the fires, and schoolteachers acted quickly to ensure their safety. An entry from the journal of the head teacher of Lauderdale School, near the Rokeby area, reads: "This afternoon a fierce fire was seen approaching the school from the Rokeby area. A decision was made to **evacuate** the school to the beach as there was doubt in my mind as to whether the school would be safe."

Who started the fires?

Investigations concluded that, of the 110 fires known to have been burning that morning, only 22 fires started accidentally. Eight started as **spot fires**. The other 14 started for a number of different reasons, such as sparks escaping from fires at garbage dumps or **incinerators**. The rest of the fires had been deliberately set.

Why were the fires set?

Most of the fires were set for **land management**. Some were started to clear ground in order to encourage new growth for animals to feed on. Some were set to get rid of **inflammable** debris from forest floors.

Firefighters clear a firebreak in a forested area.

In some cases, it was impossible to see why fires were started, leading investigators to believe that at least of few must have been set as acts of **arson**.

Bushfires

Some **bushfires** are caused by natural events, such as lightning. However, most are caused by human carelessness, such as dropping a lighted match. Australians are constantly reminded to be careful with fires. In rural areas, volunteers are trained to be firefighters. **Firebreaks** are cleared. Also, fire-spotting towers dot the landscape. Summer is a dangerous time. Not only is the area dry and hot, but many tourists may not be aware of the fire hazards.

Recognizing Dangers

Many fires are caused by carelessness. The fires you have read about in this book show that even minor mistakes can be disastrous.

House fires

The danger of a house fire is that it can grow very quickly. Once it takes hold, it is often unstoppable. Poisonous gases and smoke collect inside a building. The fire creates intense heat. A typical house fire can burn at 6000°F (3,300°C). Heat like this can ignite walls and furniture many feet away from the original fire. A house can become an **inferno** in minutes.

"During the early stages of a fire, the signs can be quite small," says Professor David Purser of England's Building Research Establishment. "Even when they become more obvious, people may just carry on what they were doing and put themselves in extreme danger. One of the problems is that people don't often recognize how fast fires can grow."

A small fire can grow rapidly to become an uncontrollable blaze that kills hundreds of people or engulfs a building in minutes.

Modern firefighters use power hoses and long, extendable ladders to extinguish a house fire.

A standard house smoke alarm can save lives.

Limiting the risks

What makes fire so dangerous is the way people ignore the risks. People often don't take fire seriously enough until it is too late. For example, many people don't bother to install smoke alarms, even though they are inexpensive and life-saving. Fire is not predictable, but plans can be made to fight it. Equipment such as **fire extinguishers** or water hoses can be kept on hand. Fire risks, such as piles of trash, can be cleared away. People can be trained. Buildings can be designed so that people can get out quickly if a fire occurs.

Invisible danger

In most house fires, people are not killed by the flames, but by smoke and gas. Carbon monoxide (CO) is particularly deadly. This colorless, odorless, invisible gas is responsible for most fire deaths. It can kill in minutes. Most victims fall unconscious without ever knowing what happened.

Simple smoke alarms are the best way to avoid being overcome by the smoke and gas produced by fire. Most alarms cannot detect CO (though some are specially designed to do this), but they do warn of the smoke that a fire produces with gases like CO. Fire safety experts recommend that all families have working smoke alarms in their homes.

The World's Worst Fire Disasters

There have been many thousands of fire disasters around the world. Those listed here are a selection of some of the worst, chosen because of the destruction they caused or the number of lives that were lost.

Rome, July 18, A.D. 64 Ten of Rome's fourteen regions are destroyed or badly damaged by fire.

Great Fire of London, September 2–5, 1666 Fire destroys 13,200 houses and 87 **parish** churches. 100,000 people become homeless. It is thought that only eight people are killed.

La Compania Church, Santiago, Chile, December 8, 1863 A lamp catches fire during a service and the church burns. Over 2,500 people are trapped inside and killed.

The Great Chicago Fire, October 8–10, 1871 A fire spreads quickly through the city, killing about 300 people and destroying 100,000 homes.

Hamburg, Germany, July 25–28, 1943 World War II bombing creates a fire that kills 45,000 people and destroys the city.

Dresden, Germany, February 13–17, 1945 Bombing raids during World War II create a firestorm that kills between 150,000 and 400,000 people. The city is destroyed.

Tokyo, Japan, March 9–10, 1945 Bombing raids during World War II create a firestorm that kills between 80,000 and 200,000 people. The city is destroyed.

Tasmanian bushfires, Australia, February 7, 1967 The "Black Tuesday" **bushfires** destroy over 1,400 homes and kill 62 people.

Grand Hotel, Las Vegas, Nevada, November 21, 1980 Fire in a hotel and casino kills 100 people and injures 600 others.

Salang Pass Tunnel, Afghanistan, November 2, 1982 Fire breaks out after a crash in a mountain tunnel. Between 1,000 and 2,700 people are trapped inside and suffocated.

Ash Wednesday fires, Australia, February 16, 1983 Bushfires destroy hundreds of homes and kill 83 people.

Bradford City Football Stadium, England, May 11, 1985 56 people die in a fire in the stadium; 70 are injured.

Kuwait, February–November 1991 Over 700 oil wells are burned by retreating Iraqi troops during the Gulf War.

Mandi Dabwali, India, December 23, 1995 Fire in a school tent kills 500 people.

Indonesia, 1997 Bushfires burn up to a million acres of forest across Indonesia. Fogs of smoke affect up to 70 million people in countries across the region.

Seen from space!

Fires in Amazonia are raging constantly as rain forest is burned and cleared. The smoke from these fires can even be seen from space!

32 people died in a fire at this underground train station in London on November 18, 1987.

Glossary

architect person who designs buildings

arson when a fire is lit on purpose with the intention of causing damage to people or property

Assemblyman old-fashioned word for a person who is part of a law-making council

bushfire fire in a forest or shrub area, usually widespread

combustible describes a material that burns easily

dousing pouring large amounts of water onto a fire to put it out

drought long period without rain when land becomes very dry

ember smoldering piece of wood or coal from a fire

evacuate to move people from a dangerous place until the danger is over

firebreak open space of land, cleared of trees and other plantlife. The fire cannot cross the cleared area as there is no fuel to burn.

fire door door made out of fire-resistant materials to keep a fire from spreading in a building

fire extinguisher container with a jet to spray liquid foam, chemicals or water to put out a fire

humidity amount of moisture in the air

inferno intense, uncrontrollable fire

incinerator furnace or other container used for burning trash

inflammable catching fire easily

island state island that is not a separate country but is part of a country on the mainland

land management taking action to manage the land in a way that benefits people and the environment

loot to steal goods from buildings that have been abandoned because of disaster or war

meteorologist person who studies and forecasts the weather

militia military force made up of civilians

parish area that has its own church. In England, land was divided this way for the purposes of local government.

pitch sticky, black tar-like substance

spot fire fire started by burning embers blown in the wind

thatch roof covering made of straw, reeds, or a similar material

tinder very dry wood used to light fires

whirlwind mass of air or fire which whirls around quickly

More Books to Read

Duey, Kathleen. *Fire: Chicago, 1871*. Madison, Wis.: Demco Media, 1998.

Knapp, Brian. *Fire*. Austin, Tex.: Raintree Steck-Vaughn Publishers, 1990.

Robbins, Ken. *Fire*. New York: Henry Holt & Company, LLC, 1995.

Index